55 DEVOTIONALS (AGAINST ERASURE)

Andrew McDonnell was born in Shoreham, Kent, in 1977. He writes poetry and fiction and has written a Creative Writing handbook, *Our Story Needs Your Story: Writing Working Class Experience* (Story Machine, 2026). He lives in Norwich but lectures at University Centre Peterborough in English Literature and Creative Writing.

Also by Andrew McDonnell

Our Story Needs Your Story: Writing Working Class Experience (Story Machine, 2026)

The Somnambulist Cookbook   (Salt, 2019)

CONTENTS

This book is dedicated to my parents, Michael and Frances, and my maternal grandmother Marie, who gave me and my sisters, Anna and Jennifer, so much love.

It is also dedicated to my children Chloe and Charlie.

Thank you to C.S. Tait for reading, listening and suggesting edits.
I am always in your fealty.

ISBN: 978-1-917617-58-1

Cover designed by Aaron Kent

Cover image: © Arteria|lab / Adobe Stock

Edited and Typeset by Aaron Kent

Broken Sleep Books Ltd
PO BOX 102
Llandysul
SA44 9BG

55 Devotionals (Against Erasure)

Andrew McDonnell

Broken Sleep Books

To resist assimilation is to insist on our working-class origins, on carrying with us the lives and histories of our families, communities, histories, and culture. To give up pretending that one is not who one is, is to render one's self marginalized.

— Cynthia Cruz, *The Melancholia of Class*

DEVOTIONAL FOR A WRITING MANIFESTO

All we need is here on earth. The little things have the answers, in the slants and the edges of the edges of our lives. Your story is our story. My story is our story. It has a place amongst all their stories that push their way to the front noisily. They jab pens into us as they pass. The stories we will tell are full of tiny stabbings. We recover our wounded from their erasers, from the stories that push them down into the fibres of the page where they cannot be read. *White trash. Grotesques. Gritty.* Holograms are all we are beneath their pens. *What did your father do for a living when you were twelve?* We plug the stab wounds with words, with experience, and we begin the process of writing what is erased. Putting the world back together. This is not sanctification. This is elbow room in the dark. This is pushing off the foot that holds the head beneath the waterline. Let this light take back the space. Let them know we are coming for them with words that are alive. Words that make us visible. Voices that resist.

Write it.

DEVOTIONAL FOR A MILK FLOAT

Every day the milk float passed the same spot at the same time. Is that devotion? And when the Carter boy was run over, outside the little shop, pockets full of pink fondant shrimps in a pink and white paper bag, he lay on the road utterly devoted to the absurdity of milk floats which were silenced by the edgeland supermarkets draining the pink tits of cows at a faster demand, so that one day he could lie in bed devoted and tell his love that he was one of the last men to be run over by a milk float; his tiny stab at immortality, and the glass bottles still clinking like a dog awaiting its beating.

DEVOTIONAL FOR WALKING

On walks, we are free. Nearly. The footpaths we take are between fields or private woodland or beside orchards. In case we feel these boundaries to be ambiguous, nailed to trees are signs telling us that what lies beyond is

PRIVATE
KEEP OUT!

When the red flags fly at the MOD rifle range, we cannot cross the line between life and death. My eldest sister couldn't get a job at Fort Halstead. Our Irish surname too much of a risk to the security of this green and pleasant land and the nuclear testing deep beneath the chalk of the western down. This is, we are told in school, our Albion, even us with a 'paddy' surname. I am not so sure. We are just borrowing what's beneath our feet. We are neither one thing nor the other. My dad can tell me who owned what. Whose woods these are, he thinks he knows. The original small tithings eroded by mechanical farming. This is not nature, this is a factory where each field is someone's bottom line, with engineered and taxable crops, but I love my dad and all that matters is that we are nearly free.

TRESSPASSERS WILL BE
PROSECUTED

My sisters one day turn to me, near the private track we trespass down to the stream at Home Farm. They tell me how pleased Dad is to have a son, as now our name can continue. I see a shire horse, a heavy bridle around its neck. I drag our name down the stubbly field. It ploughs an Irish furrow into English ground.

DEVOTIONAL FOR A 19TH CENTURY BATTLESHIP OFF THE COAST OF KENT

I am a ship that carries my ancestors off to battle. They are a hardy crew. Jock can undo a knot with his teeth. Tall Seamus can load the cannon despite being half the height of the rest of the lads. The waves lift and drop us like our mammy to the breast. There are so many of us we may not tally when we come home. *We're all at sea,* Margate Sydney the ship's bookie jokes, but I can't hear anyone else laughing, only the sea spraying this ship of boys shouting into the English Channel and the wind hitting them around the face with their accents until they sink deep in the waters of my glottal stops.

DEVOTIONAL FOR FOUR MEN STANDING IN A FIELD

I stood in the field with the men. My father to my right. Harold Dinnis to my left. Some other man who in this moment has become forgotten. (Sorry old boy). It is harvest and there is a mutton grey sky beyond a gammon pink horizon. The crop has gone for another year and the stubble is hard to walk upon with little legs. Dinnis kicks something over with his heavy boot. A family of field mice make a break for it. In the company of men, no one speaks of these beautiful things, for these moments are commonplace and they are not what us men speak of. What we did speak of I cannot remember, like the fourth man, I tell you, all these years later.

DEVOTIONAL FOR WOODLICE

Animals surround us. Deer in the headlights. The fox we fed that Vin up the road shot. Roman snails, escapees from the pots at Lullingstone Roman Villa, their shells white from the chalk of the downs. Hoverflies in the shade of the cooking apple tree waiting to raid the aphids the ants are farming all around. The petroleum sheen of the slowworms who live in the compost heap. This is the boy naturalist's kingdom. Flora and fauna have no Latin names here. They are logged and recorded by our idiomatic taxonomies. Birdsong belongs to little Jenny Wren or Cock Robin. Beyond the world of pets, other things move inside the family home. A flea might land upon the arm when the cats have been socialising, or flies may ride the summer thermals in the centre of the living room, their sharp angles spelling out the language of flies. However, it is the woodlouse, (cheesy bug. Inf) that concerns me. Isopods that were here long before us and have adapted to our pebbledash and wood-chip. They have no interest in this smaller biped who traces their passage through the forest and open heaths of the carpet to some crack in the skirting board that they know leads them into the walls of the house. Poorly ventilated homes, the gift to these crustaceans and their water dousing antennae. Wise old men of armour and free from want. They coil up if I try to touch them. Always on the way to somewhere. Always busy like the sad adults who have no time to stop and look at things with a child's eye. Who turn wistful when the small boy naturalist reminds them that there is wonder. And it is free.

DEVOTIONAL FOR A CARE HOME IN WILMINGTON

Plastic Christmas trees and plastic chairs. Plastic backing tracks of Christmas hits to sing along to in the canteen. A man called Guy with bleached mullet who is a hit with his charges knows all the tunes to bring a little joy. The curved walls of corridors and room after room after room of lives behind numbered doors. Here is my Aunt who made it to the middle-classes. A former head teacher, she was evicted from private care after dancing naked one Christmas in front of the other residents. Now she's returned to council care and the working classes who sing along with Guy. It's the 1980s and she spends her hours in the large day room where no-one speaks. Just beyond the dismal hedges is the heath and home to the Dartford warbler, a near-threatened species. Maybe taught Mick 'n' Keef how to sing. The centre of its belly a dirty white patch. Its song not yet erased.

DEVOTIONAL FOR THE MOTORWAY BRIDGE AT SWANLEY BEFORE THE M25 CONNECTED IT

Many years ago, at the Swanley interchange, a bridge stood with no road at either end. Nearby was the KA factory where my grandmother ran grooves into her palms from holding a soldering iron eight hours a day, making circuit boards for unimaginable things.

From her work-bench, she once watched three children balance along the metal edge of the safety barrier. Yellow dandelions dirtied and swaying in the lorry winds.

DEVOTIONAL FOR A NATURALISATION

Great Grandfather Theodor from Bornholm became British in 1912. German but from Danish soil, this sleight of hand protected him from both war and internment, a blur in the identity parade of aliens and friends to the King and the Union. His son, my grandfather Theo, was not so lucky. He was made a sniper in the second war. He was always left behind to pick off any advancing German line, his hands on the gun. That's all we know, that's all he must have said, as that's all my grandmother said, as that's all my mum told me. He refused to collect his medals, but he did play the violin, his hands bowing the strings in their little living room in Swanley. There are only small things I remember. The brown leather buttons of his cardigan. Those same hands that shot men and played music, lifting me gently upwards and onto his knees, those buttons twisting in my fingers like tuning a radio, searching for a wavelength I can settle.

DEVOTIONAL FOR FOOD

My maternal grandmother filled her larder with sweet things and fed me with love. So much joy in the refinement of sugar. Fizzy drinks. Cola-floats. Hours divided by chocolate and French Fancies. It is cheap. It is in plenty. It is my hit. I am a junk, according to the father of a middle-class friend who knows what a junk is from Radio4. I am a boat for sugar swept up at their table. But not just a boat. I am too a magnet for wasps. I am a spoke in the cycle of deprivation.

She would never touch potatoes. When she had her own babies during rationing, she was so malnourished she could not breastfeed. All they ate were potatoes *stolen from the surrounding fields*, she said, as her fingers tapped the table as if trying to dig into the teak.

My metformin gently hum in their blister packs.

DEVOTIONAL FOR A PROBLEM OF MASCULINITY

My dad had an old steel toolbox and one Christmas we gave him a Black and Decker workbench to replace the thing that could take off a finger when it folded. As men - boy and man - we both took great joy in the possibilities of things that could be realised on this bench. It spoke to us as men. It called to us as men. In truth, it was used by him to saw some wood to go up in the kitchen and then just became something else to hang coats on.

When he got a job as a sales rep for a farming company, he sometimes took me into the office. We might pop down to the stores, where men in blue work jackets and ponytails stood behind a counter. These were the masters of a galaxy of spare parts, pipes and bolts and male and female fittings. Here, on the wall behind them were agricultural calendars of semi-naked women draped across bailers, with perms like my mother did for the old women in the village. With their jaded lust, they looked out at us boys looking at them from the bailers, and the cabs of combine harvesters and Fordson tractors. Shaking like the wheat before the blade.

DEVOTIONAL FOR A PROBLEM OF MASCULINITY

We are the men on a Saturday morning, reading the magazines for free in WH Smith on the high street. It's what us men do on Saturday mornings: we drive into town to access reading material. We sometimes take Andrew Munday if he's lucky. I paw and pore over Whizzer and Chips, The Beano, the cartoon spin off magazines from American culture, while my dad and whoever has cadged a lift read about steam trains or whatever manly things they can on a wet Saturday morning. We are not alone, there are many men here with no intent of buying, just standing in silence reading as a way to pass the minutes of our lives. This is how us men access literature. Outside the high street is full of wives and sisters, shifting between Boots and the hairdressers, feeling guilty for making us wait, the smell of rain and leaded petrol perfuming their necks, banging on the window for their men to take them home.

DEVOTIONAL FOR MY GRANDMOTHER'S HANDS

We don't know the last time we will enter a house. My grandmother lived on Willow Avenue. Her house sat on the turning circle. People cared about their gardens. They would keep their box hedge the same height. Complement the colours of each other's gardens with flowers fat with bees and cabbage whites. The road was never properly laid. It was ridged and between each poured slab was a rubbery join that melted each summer. It was owned by the council and after her final fall, what was left was boxed up and what wasn't wanted was taken to the tip. We don't know the last time we will enter a house. By the back door there were marks where we were measured: crude biro lines scribbled above heads that went up and up until eventually the recording stopped. When she was dying, I held her hand and thought hard about that hand. I recorded the lines on the palm. I recorded the lines on her fingers, the vertical lines, the horizontal lines. I recorded the feeling of her cool skin against my skin. I recorded the back of her hand, how her wedding band sat on her finger, her engagement ring leaning in for support. I recorded the weight of her hand in mine. I recorded how much smaller it was. I recorded the little tightening of her grip, and then I stopped recording and just sat with her. Always be on standby to record. We don't know the last time we will enter a house.

DEVOTIONAL FOR A SOFA BED

Every night after I had gone to bed. After my sisters had gone to bed. After my grandmother had gone to bed. After the flies that landed on her thick tights had gone to bed. After the dog had gone to bed. The goldfish in their tank. The cats and their fleas. The TV. The Gilham's next door. (The closing of doors everywhere). My parents would unfold the green sofa into their bed, and once inside the dog and the cats would curl up at their feet, like statues of the dead laid out in cathedrals.

On cold mornings, before my father had made the fire, I would creep into the warmth of their bed. Not once did they send me back. I was an expensive alarm clock set to doze for ten minutes between them, and soon my father would be up making us a mug of tea with a Bourbon biscuit to tide us over til breakfast. As my mum put away their bedding in the boiler cupboard, and folded their bed back into a green sofa, my father would gently remove the ash from yesterday's fire on the metal pan with remnants of heat glowing in the first light before bringing down his mother's bedpan of unmentionables to be flushed away.

And then the opening of doors everywhere.

DEVOTIONAL FOR A HILL

then we came on foot by Latham's farm

the light is blue; the fields hold a quality of cold

that haunts our walking man and boy

along the edge of wood and field where the hill drops

down a fox skirts the orange brush

a stain of something which silences

in Maidstone hospital I read to him

poems with trains - the charge of Whitsun Weddings,

the pausing of Adlestrop -

like moments we shared when

I was young and that long ago fox

enters the clinical light

now my son sits on my knee

my father and that fox are gone

we chase them in the gloom of a standard lamp

as outside snow falls over the city

Dad's flat cap on the floor as if he melted

my son holding tightly onto me

DEVOTIONAL FOR WALKING

It was a magical thing where the path split in the wood and my father said one day when we have time we'll go by Shepherd's Barn, when your legs can carry you further and the light is not against us. It haunted the edges of my mind, like suburban lanes waiting for developers.

We made it there when I was five. A clapboard shack where a farmhand once took his life. I remember one light-bulb, nothing else, shining between the planks that had slipped, one glass window, pines behind. Mist moved across the bracken as our breath forged tiny ghosts in the November air.

Now it's the M25.

DEVOTIONAL FOR TARMAC

In the late 1950s the motorways came, and my dad answered the calling. He left behind the plough and furrow to build the roads of tomorrow. All across the land men like him downed their tools and knelt before the gods of tarmacadam. They became masters of the machines, the white heat radiating out from beneath their yellow hard hats like pipe smoke in Whitehall planning rooms. The roads they built connected them together. Interlocked postcodes ushered in new estates and industrial parks. Old Albion hidden behind deep banks and hump-back bridges and ancient woodland glowing in the light of Happy Eaters. And so, our family holidays became a thing, a thing that was spent during two weeks in summer on some farmyard caravan site. We ate in the silence of the future on plastic chairs, off plastic plates at Formica tables with plastic cutlery, listening to the rain of England drumming its psalms on the canvas of the awning. My dad planning our day-trips on steam trains across moorland to a past he had unknowingly helped make redundant.

DEVOTIONAL FOR A SWIMMING IMPROVEMENT CUP

They had to give us something, something to mark
the end of our passage through the village school.
On the table various shields and large cups, and at
the back the smaller ones. On the shield were smaller
silver shields, engraved with the names of the middle
classes. What bright futures awaited them at grammar
school? What expectations did they have placed upon
them? Then the smaller cups for us 11+ failures, the
Did well at reading cup, the *Helped at the dinner hall cup*,
and mine, *the Swimming Improvement Cup*, awarded to
me for not drowning. There is a photo of me holding
it, wonky front teeth, a body growing at different rates,
the uncertainty in my eyes like a dog in a locked car.
My name engraved in 8pt, so they could get another
ten years of us on it and above me another 11+ failure
from the estate who also failed to drown. Sure enough,
the following year it went to a girl in Mildmay Place.
We were winners me and them, and every day the
kids who won the shields could watch as I went from
door-to-door stuffing papers through their letterboxes.
The weight of the paper bag like walking through deep
water, then the feeling of them standing on me to keep
their own heads above the surface.

DEVOTIONAL FOR A PROBLEM OF MASCULINITY

My father was the tower captain, and I was soon to give up. 15 and enchanted by the sound of grunge/grebo/ motorik, rather than summoned by bells. There was a moment, on the way to the belfry one Sunday morning - in the cab of a farmer who saw us walking - where my dad in the three seats we sat in, placed his arm around me with pride. It felt odd, the weight of his arm. It was the first time he had found a way to express his love in this way and I did not know what to do with it, as if he had broken the puzzle of his own absent father.

DEVOTIONAL FOR A PROBLEM OF MASCULINITY

I am built to be scary. *Stand up for yourself. Hit them back.* But what could I do? I was a bookish lump, so happy in a way that I was still to learn to hide from others, because this is not a happy world, and happiness is not infectious. My dad whistled when he was happy. He was always whistling. His whistling was a weapon in this unhappy world. But he knew how to be handy if it came to it, if push followed shove. That whistle carried something in its cadences, it coiled around him like fire. But my paws were made for eating honey, my voice for poetry. When I found the Puffin anthology *Voices*, I hid it in my school bag.

One night at the station, a group of boys threatened us. They laid into the long hair metal lads. My father was picking us up and went round to the boot of the car where he stored his orange handled bowie knife. My friend, seventeen years old, calmly touched his arm and said to leave it, as the chaos of violent boys and men spiralled all around us.

DEVOTIONAL FOR THE ARTS

At home we all have different tastes in the arts. My uncle paints watercolours of steam trains for my father to hang on the walls of our house. My mother draws faces on the telephone pad. She would have gone to art school, but her parents refused. My paternal grandmother has a print of a Victorian child mesmerised by bubbles. It is tiny and hangs in the corner above the plug for the television. One sister has a Pierrot clown weeping. Another Steinlen's *Le Chat Noir*. I have a book on Warhol's Factory. *That's not art though*, I'm told by the other boys who know fine art. The boys in my art class paint tasteful still life. Baked beans cascade out of a famous brand. Flowers wilt in glass vases refracting afternoon light that falls *just-so*. Fruit flirts in their mother's decorative salad bowls. It takes them weeks to complete. My own art is sixth-form abstract expressionism that are done on a photocopier and completed in an hour. They tut and tell me I'll probably go far. I write lines of poetry over the abstract faces and patterns. One of the art teachers looks deep into my work on display beside the still life then takes me to one-side. Touching my elbow, she asks, *Is everything alright at home?*

DEVOTIONAL FOR MY SCHOOL UNIFORM

Mum had boiled it, blazer, trousers, shirts, the lot and
all we had was £50 from the housekeeping - there were
no supermarket uniforms in 1990. A day off from school
on a train gliding to Bromley through spring sunlight, a
rare moment of just the two of us in stolen hours. Army
& Navy, C&A, various department stores and ill-fitting
blazers or trousers too long in the leg. *Uniforms level
up poverty*. At the Wildernesse School for Boys, wealth
found other ways via early 1990s fashion: the sports-
bags, the ski-jackets, Danny Warne's red Fila he wore
for four days before the rules took him back to black.
How in awe we were.

It took all day to find a fit, and when we did, we were
a few-bob short. And *oh*, how the woman took pity on
us at the till, supposing she could do it *just this time*, and
a look at me from her (in store uniform), as if I were
an annoyance. Something that made her day harder.
That train ride home - a humiliation between us and
the discounted uniform.

DEVOTIONAL FOR MRS BINHAM'S SHY DAUGHTER

Through the lichgate I lead Mrs Binham's shy daughter and into the church to take a pew. The choir are gone and, in their place, an orchestra. The vicar, spectacled, a flush of black hair, starts them off like a mid-century band leader and it's so beautiful I cry. Tim and Wendy bang on the window, hold a sign up saying 'you said it started at 7:30'. The shy daughter lets go of my hand, for she's appalled I saved all this sadness for myself and denied my friends their tears. To appease I go outside and try to explain to them what I heard, but it's impossible and it's gone. Now the shy daughter has gone, and the church is empty. Oh, how I had wanted, in silence, to brush the curls from her face and stare into those black eyes and sing her songs of mountains, but now she's gone and I am a disappointment just as her mother had warned. I see them now, at the vanity dresser, hairbrush in Mrs Binham's hand, smiling in her grief, humming tunelessly as she straightens each of her shy daughter's curls for better men to come.

DEVOTIONAL FOR A GAP YEAR

1996 and in the doldrums where nothing moves me. My middle-class friends are spending their gap years being held at knifepoint in India. Catching Greyhound coaches with strangers confiding in them about murders as they cross America. Crashing mopeds in Thailand. I am on a Mezzanine floor of a staple manufacturer on an industrial estate, stuffing archives with old orders in winter light so I can earn money for university. I am an office jockey, making mistakes and becoming overweight. I escape in lo-fi. The two note melodies on a Farfisa. The ripples of a Moog. Krautrock in a Kentish landscape. Bands with names like Quickspace Supersport tilting me weird and carrying my head where it needs to go to escape proforma invoices and sexist jokes made by middle-aged men. My gap year peers will be lawyers. Architects. Captains of industry. I'm chasing the dreams of poetry. Because that's all I have. That's all I need. Each night it pours out of me: all the strangeness, all the glimpses of things I cannot live, all the rawness of being nineteen and knowing the home is surrounded by places to go if only you can afford it. So, there I lie on my bedroom floor and write it all in blue ink on a bumper jotter stolen from work. I write my gap year, sponsored by Bic.

DEVOTIONAL FOR CULTURAL STUDIES

After the seminar on Raymond Williams, we lunch in the student union. *You're middle-class now*, X tells me. He looks to my shoulder to see if the chip he imagines sits there has fallen away. I protest but he has prepared for this debate. *As soon as you go to university,* he tells me, *you have risen to become a product of Thatcher's trickle-down economics.* I can't afford lunch, but I am allowed a cup of tea under his fiscal observations. I have no sensible answers. I can't pass for middle-class, not with my accent. He is erasing me, and I am a haunted house being gentrified. My inner wallpaper and Axminster carpet whorls will be reappropriated in tasteful beige. Rather than compartmentalised, I will now have a narrative flow. Raymond Williams is still on his bus riding from country to town. The bus is full of haunted houses. It passes many haunted houses, all dark mirrors reflecting more dark mirrors. Boarded up, still waiting for a trickle of piss to reach them.

DEVOTIONAL FOR HOUSE-SITTING

After graduation I often felt a loss: the world which had suddenly expanded was now compressed to call centres above ring roads, water cooler politics, warnings about getting above the station you were born into. Sometimes, I was a house-sitter in a five-storey-pile with cats. I sat in the semi-dark of their bathroom watching the moon in the empty tub. I had no way to express what I felt - too young and in limbo to put it down - the woman who owned the place advised me people always come back around to find a place in our lives somehow. That what we had experienced never goes away. I didn't see her for years after that, but I kept thinking about what she said and when I got round to asking after her, they told me she was dead.

DEVOTIONAL FOR A BIANCHI BICYCLE

The first thing I ever bought myself of any value was a Bianchi bicycle. I was in my thirties and teaching adults in a county council education service, and I could sacrifice some salary for something special and so beautiful it made my heart ache. My thirties bought me things my earlier life could not support. A laptop of my own. Decent shoes. Holidays that were not staying with my parents for a week. (This is not a complaint). This is a love poem for a bicycle. Something that felt like the first thing precious I had given myself. See, there's miles and miles and miles legs can turn to feel free. The first thirty miles clear life, the arguments lost, the things we should have done differently, and then the second thirty are free from these thoughts, and you are just turning, turning, turning the chain. Then the final thirty are coming back with all those miles like a secret love affair buried deep to face the same faces and pettiness of life. To lean the bike against the wall and tell myself all it gave me was mine, and no-one could take it away from me.

DEVOTIONAL FOR CORAL BRIDGES AND OTHER MIDDLE-CLASS SOFT-ESTATES

This is your time of arrival: past walk-in wardrobes, past ornamental wishing-wells, where roller blinds of unimaginable colours green at the edges, where crazy-paving is a mess of weeds beneath the sadness of summer. Here you can recall the lost hobbies of residents such as mossy terrarium management, walking closed bus routes, moving on groups of youths with Sharpies from the recreation ground memorial bench where animals cross from their world into ours. On the hill you can look to the soft estate of Coral Bridges beyond your own and hear the sound of teenage sons of GP fathers practise their drums in garages at the end of long drives. Where the same fathers warn their daughters about boys like you as you fold their broadsheets and push them through their metal letter boxes. When you enter Coral Bridges, you go against yourself, as if you are being constantly observed.

You left something in Coral Bridges from your own estate, the image of girls on June lawns cutting each other's hair; the seaweed of wet hair curling against a Minnie Mouse towel. Of people laughing and fixing their cars on a Saturday afternoon. Your parents as target silhouettes in their kitchen windows.

DEVOTIONAL FOR AN IRON BRIDGE

We go down to the iron bridge and the river. We go down together to stand in the stone stream. The horses in the paddock come and go. We go down to the iron bridge. The dogs go down to the iron bridge to stand in the stone stream. Our dogs come and go. The iron bridge has holes. The iron has panels. Panels rust down by the stream. Panels bend and become holes. We go down to see the holes. See the light of the river dance against the iron beneath the bridge. Here is a photograph of Dad who went down to the iron bridge. He is ten and has a jam jar to dip into the stream. He turns his head to look into the lens. The other boys look down into the water. Dads come and go. Do the same particles of water ever pass through the same place twice? We go down to the iron bridge. There are different horses in the paddock. Here are little boys who have gone down to the iron bridge for a birthday. Our mothers sit on blankets under the shade. Mothers come and go. We wade downstream. Particles of water fill our Wellington boots. Boys come and go. We go down to the iron bridge. It is concrete now. I stand and look down beneath the shade of the tree. My son has water in his wellingtons. He looks up. The dog beside him looks up.

DEVOTIONAL FOR MY FOUR-YEAR OLD SINGING TO HIMSELF IN THE BATHROOM ALONE

I can hear him now he's singing to his heart's content the starry firmament of LEDs above him the cold tiles beneath the feet the constellations of mould around the edges of the stuff you squeeze to stop the water leaking down the back of the bath *it's not the purple hills / it's not the silver lake* and he is singing for he is happy he is in his own private space thinking nothing of the government of the people out there that are dying right now no know this that he is so very full of life his joyous little voice carries something in it that we can honestly call joy with such certainty here in a world of such uncertainty.

For me it is echoes of myself singing to my heart's content in the cold toilet at the end of the house above me the flimsy remains of cobwebs covered in soot from coal carried in through the back door past bags of potatoes waiting to be pressed through the chipper this singing is never as free as free as in these moments.

DEVOTIONAL FOR A PROBLEM OF MASCULINITY

Me and my kids, we went to Foxley Woods after restrictions had been removed and the grasses were so tall that my son had to be carried through on my shoulders. *I'm just a little boy* he said, riding up there, and I strode on, briefly a champion of the afternoon. *I once wrestled a goat for you,* I thought, took it by the horns and pushed the fucker back to the wall. Those eyes with rectangled desire for the sandwiches I had made. How manly I am, wrestling a goat. How strong and fearless as I calmly walk through the storm. *But I'm just a little boy* I thought, *just a little boy.*

DEVOTIONAL FOR THE ACLE STRAIGHT

Farmland passes on the horizon, the soft smoke of a sugar beet factory hangs above the flatland and seems to move at the pace of the coach. Orange curtains hang against the snow, the purple of the fields and the frozen puddles of water that I can imagine my dead dad's ghost breaking with his walking stick.

Worldly things seem so brittle, so precarious: the television masts, the fleet of white hire vans surrounded by floodlights, the two-carriage train high on the bank. We pass single drivers going the other way, the coach driver catching one last look at them in his side mirrors. Behind us, Great Yarmouth is lighting its lights against the coming tides.

DEVOTIONAL FOR A SEAL AT WAXHAM

Little son of mine fell face down in the brine. He is soaked and I pull the t-shirt with a skeleton skateboarding, and then the vest with contrasting colours of public transport in miniature, up and off like papery skin from garlic, until his perfect trunk is under the sun. Those little arms and shoulders somehow supporting the large head with the whirlpool crown now covered in sand.

There, in the water, a bowling ball head with fat currants for eyes, rises from out the depths and stares at us from the sweeping waves. I am open mouthed, agog. My boy shives the hole in the surface with his sobs. It comes close, warns us off, sinks and is gone.

DEVOTIONAL FOR 3.5-THOUSAND-YEAR-OLD FROG

In the grand scale of things, it was probably made an hour before we arrived to gawp at it through glass. When we were driving in my car someone unknown hurtled through their life and made this little cream frog crouched in time for us to find on our list of things we write to keep the smaller one out of the gift shop. *When I was your age,* I say, *in the living room, we all had our corners.* I could be found at the end of the sofa on the floor, an outrider for alerting the family that the cats had fleas again. Behind us, my mother draped in my sisters, my dad in his chair, his mother in hers, and behind them, the glass display cabinet on which the fish tank sat. Beneath a porcelain donkey in grey and white, smooth with big old eyes, sat behind finger marked transparency, our little stab at stillness in a house that was always moving. The donkey is lost to time. *We don't expect to see him here,* I tell them. *Let's look harder,* they say.

DEVOTIONAL FOR A HILL

When my son was young and coming to mine, he would fall asleep in the car, and I'd carry him up to bed. I went the long way round, dropping down a steep hill, as that was the point he would always go off, as if the sudden feeling of being weightless made his consciousness a balloon floating out of his hands to rest against the sunroof beneath the night. I can't remember when that simple feeling of dropping stopped working for me, when the weight finds us. Do you remember when you could no longer be carried to bed, when you had to work your own way to it?

In those early days of being alone again, especially when the kids were with their mother, I'd come to in my rented rooms, and wonder in my confusion if my parents were downstairs waiting for me, to ruffle my hair, or just look up to audit my existence, their voices falling away, down and down into the silent house.

DEVOTIONAL FOR A PATIO

In the cathedral, awkwardly we light candles for my father. I don't know what I am supposed to feel, it's just another flame flickering in the ambulatory. It doesn't tell how he built roads or ploughed fields. All that is erased. All that is always erased. Years ago, I worked in a bar with a large patio at the back. A man sat there wistful and when I passed, he told me how he had laid all these stones. I was in my twenties and didn't care for the impermanence of things. You feel like your days go on forever. All he wanted was some acknowledgment that these concrete squares I swept, I pressure washed, I stubbed out my fags on, were down to him, and how hard it had been to get them to sit flat. I was complicit in erasure, and he knew it as his tone turned bitter. Now we light little candles for my father and countless men and women like him, and I stumble towards some sort of half-hearted penance. My son leads us into the lady chapel, tells us to sit and his little face becomes serious in the Decembered cathedral. His sister and I look at each other as he sits there in his thoughts, and I wonder what it is I cannot feel.

DEVOTIONAL FOR WEST STOW ANGLO SAXON VILLAGE

The skull of the Anglo-Saxon man sits behind glass. Some effort has been made to reconstruct his face. It stares down from the wall as a shy teenager bottom lip slightly bit. He could be anyone's kid here today who got bored and wandered off to dream of girls or boys before getting his head caved in by some stranger that haunts the edges of these woods and dreams. The bogeyman who comes when the dog whistle is blown to take our children off to a Neverland of ideas it's hard to break them from. I imagine these men smell of piss and saloon bars. The buildings here are reconstructed with straw and shit, and the houses smell of ash and animal skin. I'm not sure what to do with all this history, it feels a stretch to say it is my roots. That these are my distant ancestors with their love for pots and swords and burying ships. I prefer the sea, the protozoic slime from which we bubbled and fucked our way out of and into the trees. England is just a haunted dancehall where the skeletons circle with empty dance cards. When we were young, there was always a danger of violence at any time. Simon, in his cardigans too big for him, was jumped by fifteen kids one Friday night we watched him go down and did nothing for fear the violence would come to us. I thought those days were gone, but here we are, divided again, meatheads on the rise, all unironic in the digital spheres. Faster we dance, faster on and on and I am father to the man, and man to the father and I don't know what to do with all this, what we drive and how to steer it. To block my son's ears to the whistling. The skull of the Anglo-Saxon man sits behind glass.

DEVOTIONAL FOR FATHERHOOD

We like the ruined castles. We can trace their shape in minutes given half the chance. The smallest leads the charge. I lollop on behind eyeing dangers he is yet to spot. The elder, she takes the middle, pivots between us like a messenger pigeon carrying news up and down the line. We pass older people, they yield to us, wave us through as they grip the rope upon the stairs. In darker corners we play the game where I am a hidden monster. I must still be me, but monstrous, something recognisable and yet somehow undead. I lift hands and death-stare straight ahead, then catch them in my arms and hold onto them as long as I can before they wriggle free and leave me behind.

DEVOTIONAL FOR THE BODY

At Sutton Hoo my son runs down the steep banks and up the other side. My daughter is wheezy with the music of her spring cold and walks beside me. Together, so she can catch her breath, we stop at many signs telling us to imagine a river busy with trade, but all I can see are the expensive yachts and sail boats of a Suffolk river town. Those ancients with their jewellery and river quests are buried beneath visitor initiatives as if we are in an Anglo-Saxon theme park. I walked here before when I was her age, but I cannot remember it. All I recall was a walk out along the Deben and seeing a yacht with beautiful naked people who all jumped into the grey light reflected on the water when they saw us in our catalogue tracksuits and ugly trainers. They had music that came in waves of notes across the still river that was paused between the tides. The memory of heat is concrete speckled with aggregate and glued together by melting tar, holding the flames of the tidal river at bay, my Garfield t-shirt covered in thunder bugs as the grimacing cat clings to my body that is becoming a stranger to me. I am older now and I cannot find the boy in the decades that have grown out from that smaller me. All these layers like a buried ship around my original body. I wonder what has happened to the bodies of those who jumped into the rivers. Do they still shimmer with the light of my imagination? Recalling the river below us and their historical moment, I now bury them in a crown of words and an older, stranger note that is always there. A little boy humming from the depths.

DEVOTIONAL FOR WALKING

My 9yo writes in her summary of January: *we went walking at the beach AGAIN!* We post it off to my mum who lives hundreds of postcodes away. Last time we spoke, her neighbour's old house, ex-council, went for over half-a-million and she wrote off her car dazzled by the sun and that her driving days were now over, but she is triple-jabbed. We walk in wellington boots. We explore the rivulets filled with shells by the retreating sea. They are never as busy as when we are on a beach. The ache of their speeding childhood walks with me. People say *what would the you of now say to the you of then*, but I am the same you. Parent, child, man, are all just masks we wear over our baby faces warped by the circus mirrors that lead in one direction. I walk to walk this off. This is all for free. The little one, he grabs his sister's hand, he grabs my hand, and says, *this is us and we love each other.* Out to sea, a little beacon on a boat flashes in the vast space and then is gone.

DEVOTIONAL FOR THE WELLS HARBOUR RAILWAY

The little train has gone that rocked

beside the long banks, where once we

rode that summer you got chickenpox.

I hear the beat of the train even now

The track has been torn up and scars

to the land are the only trace of it

how funny to feel sad about a narrow

gauge railway in days as shit as these.

It is the erasure of what's behind us

a rubber moving with precision

across the white pages of our lives.

You guys are the outriders now.

Keep going forward. Keep a beat ahead.

It's all over once you turn your head.

DEVOTIONAL FOR THE SUBJECTS OF QUEEN ELIZABETH II

Marie, my grandmother, her council house in Swanley. The fenced off pond that once held water and gave the town its name. The row of Elm that were lost to disease. The houses over at Dartford Heath that were lost this year to summer fires. What a world we live in now. I wonder if that girl from Margate would recognise it? It hit me more than I expected. It made me think of her again, how her days were lived within those days.

It hit me more than I expected. In the car with my children, the radio interrupted, I felt we were on the outside of a door sealed shut by rising waters and floating away were those who once lifted me into the air, as I now lift my children above me.

What is this lifting but a hope for the waterline to take a full lifetime to reach them?

DEVOTIONAL FOR CHILDREN'S CORNER

There in the room my dead self appears.

It is just a boy. I see him as white light

that dances by the window. Beyond

the glass the wall of the adjacent building

is covered in red leaves. The cathedral chimes

the quarter hour and I am with my own ghost.

I reach out to him and tell him it's ok

even though he cannot hear me. It's ok

I say over and over as if he is my own son

not something lost to time. I would hold

him if I could. I would lift him so he could

see the future from his little corner.

The city calls me with traffic, with late heat.

what is the adult that turns his hands

over and over, who sees the lines deepen

in cool mirrors? Whose ghosts walk beside

him in the pockets of this moment, and then

this. Then this. Tell me, what is the adult?

DEVOTIONAL FOR A HAUNTING

It's in my ears, this music,

as I cycle from one fixed point

to another

each pitch of wind sings of this land;

her ancient names, Iken, Orford, Snape

    their songs rebound from the aerials on the
ness

    a message from something erased

near the foundry at Butley Mills

three bronze figures watch over the meadows

sending back their own message,

to these unknown ghosts

    their unintendeds,

    their unannounceds:

    -w-h-e-r-e-e-v-e-r-y-o-u-

    -g-o-i-w-i-l-l-f-o-l-l-o-w-

-w-h-i-s-t-l-e-a-n-d-

                              -I'-l-l-

-c-o-m-e-to-y-o-u-

.

                    w-h-i-s-t-l-e-

        -f-o-r-u-s-a-l-l-

I sing it too with all my voice

          against the ebb tides

the message, the melody, the maps,

                              a fourth figure

who now travels without movement

          from

          one

          fixed point

                              to another

DEVOTIONAL FOR A GINGERBREAD BOY

and I am out of the oven and I hold down a job and I have sex and I make little gingerbread boys and girls and I drive a MPV and I once had a family and now I am walking out further to a place where I may no longer know the names of all I loved and the place has no name but it's in the past and I am running past my years and old men mowing their lawn wave at me like an old friend old women call to me like long forgotten children of feint muscle memories of embraces and kisses given freely of throwing love into the air waiting to catch them and one day they don't come down and I think of vanity mirrors reflecting empty streets and bay windows reflecting leafless trees and cars reflecting other bay windows and tilted vanity mirrors and I think of freshly made jam cooling in their pantries an ever present smell of dough and they will stumble across the lawn stumble across their rose beds across the mower cables and chase me down the street stop! they'll say stop little boy you look good enough to eat but I'll keep going until I am running proud on stumps and the stumps become bone and gristle staining the paths and bridleways until my grating spinal cord is worn down to chalk arrows that rain will wash away and the clever old fox sits on the riverbank waiting but I am not coming home to your jaws mister I am not coming home and one by one they return to their little griefs and large print library books and sit silent in their conservatories until the cold rises up from the floor into their bones.

DEVOTIONAL FOR A SATURDAY IN JULY

In an opening of my head where many things are entering, some take the form of slate and come towards me with their edges so the density of the stone can't be seen. Slate envelopes, I am therefore a letter box of other people's letters, but not tonight, tonight my words are a correspondence. We were at a hall and did I dream this, but there were statues and a boy lost in the long grass. People were singing to all of us, us who came in comfortable shoes, in our huddle, shadowed by sculptures of modernist design, shadowed by nettles as high as my shoulders, in this land where a man made a monument to himself. Around the Ha Ha and the giant tooth, in the mossy glade and the deep dark woods, the owls hoot, the songbirds trill, a hawk is spooked and we are carried through by voices. All I can say is that out here is something else. I don't want to go home. I have this image of you as tones. It is hard to fully explain, but I will try and take language to the edge of where it begins to breakdown. The same weekend I watched my children's sandcastle be broken by the sea. My son, he points at the waves, but says nothing as words will not stop the incoming tide. Tones are what I see when I think of you. Dots and loops, the whirl of your skirt in the gathering gloom; the juniper berries in the opaque lido of your oversized glass, our accents open to one another, no need to hide our class anymore. There is something I am trying to understand, but it only illuminates briefly in headlights as it crosses the road and vanishes back into the forest.

DEVOTIONAL FOR A PROBLEM OF MASCULINITY

I am a moving lump of cells that must follow certain rules. I must be good with my hands, plane down wood as if I were a pool attendant smoothing the surface of a lido. I confess that sometimes I dream of my children dying and I will wake and cry, but no one must know. Men don't talk about these things. Last night my dead father came to me and told me he was disappointed as what did I know about the spread of a virus? He was not my father but some devil wearing his face as my father was a good man. I try to live as him and I sometimes fail: his hat too small. My driving more erratic. What quivery pink cells I am on the motorway, shimmering in the fast lane like the windows of a distant house at midday.

DEVOTIONAL FOR A PROBLEM OF MASCULINITY

Images stretch and sounds stretch, and I connect with everything. If I were to reach out and touch you, I might give you a shock and set you on fire. You would recoil inwards like a fossil and it would begin to snow in cinemas so that the popcorn would be ruined, ice cold and wet and what do I do if our hands meet in there, and how do I know when to touch you as I would quite like to spark rather than immolate you, and it's been ever such a long time that I am terrified with all this masculinity I have, bursting at the seams as if I am a Temu Desperate Dan and I am watching the film with my eyes shut as I am terrified.

DEVOTIONAL FOR A DEAD HEDGEHOG

You spotted it, a hedgehog, dead, there above the city where the smell of fungus reigned after 3 weeks of rain. It was like a heavy duvet over us. We watched to see if it might suddenly exhale, and I thought of my father in that instant, how he let out 1 more breath as if the moment was delayed, and now here we were with a dead hedgehog where Kett mounts his rebellion 450 years ago and I am also in Maidstone hospital 3 years ago. My little girl is 8 next week and it all seems so fast that I sometimes wonder if all this is real, so I tell you and you punch my arm and now she is 12. Sometimes I have to cling to you as I am afraid I will fall, or rather float off into the air, watching you shrink into the earth. We look down at the city below, past the hedgehog, past the tree line where the river flows and wonder 50 years from now how much will be under water as the rain folds over us.

DEVOTIONAL FOR A BLACK DOG

In the yard the small boats sit on the back of trailers. Their hulls are green with mildew and there is purple in the window reflections if you stop and really look. The boats are winter vessels of the land now. They will sit like this until late spring when men with buckets and sponges will come to wash them down. Light bulbs shine from fishmonger outlets but no one is buying. The potholes are filled with rain and oil creates warped rainbows across them. The Harbour Inn sits above the flooded marshes that the October storms have filled. The lighthouse turns to the land, turns to sea, turns to land again. The tide is running water back to sea. The clouds go from here to the Netherlands. They are like flute music, a clash of shapes and notes of colour. If you listen to them, you will feel them first, their strangeness, how they surround you. How they rest upon the sea as bass notes. It is not one thing or another. The pockets of blues, the soft whites, the dark rain. Against the sky of your closed eyes a lone black dog walks the littoral. Its shape shifting as you shift to the music. It stops in the white foam wash of the sea where the sand is painted by the waves as if it has heard something barely perceptible. A whistle blown from the dunes. Calling it home. So many things felt at once. The dog turns its head as if it must decide to return and haunt the house with its dreams and its sleeping fur drying on warm stone or run on. So many things felt at once. Such strangeness. Such music. It and runs on, that black shape. It runs on. Let it go. Let it go. Open your eyes. Let go.

DEVOTIONAL FOR LOSS

Going through the long wave band on my little Panasonic, I come across the sound of birds coming into roost. The voice of the city is audible in the background, the waves of bird-wing at first seems distant then flow in so fast, so noisy, that I worry the single speaker will blow into a mess of wires, and with an unsteady hand I will push everything back in, say, *Come on, don't die just yet.* It doesn't blow and instead the wings retreat and once more spiral along the aerial before coming in for a second try, I close my eyes and concentrate on the sound and now I'm with our parents, watching them watching the birds, against a blue December sky, and while this is happening, mum says to anyone paying attention that they will move this way, they will spend their twilight hours under a Norfolk sky, much like today's. I still look at the horizon for their car. With a final twist and a few scattered the birds claim the clock tower for the night. I fold in on myself, roll the radio to off.

DEVOTIONAL FOR A PROBLEM OF MASCULINITY

There is an altar in the woods where I go and kneel on my mossy cassock. Here I play back my giddy ascent to near Alpha masculinity, learning the Greek letters in search of my station: I am Omega! I am Gamma! I am Epsilon! The internet can tell us now, where on the spectrum we sit. What kind of a man I am. But I care little for their diagnostics. I turn instead to my demigod and say, *Here, grasp my broad shoulders and ride me through the forest,* as my antlers burst from my provincial head and my little boy's body grows lean and powerful. My carcass left sitting in chip fat and sweet wrappers, wiping greasy orange fingers into Axminster whorls.

DEVOTIONAL FOR THE TRAIN AND THE RIVER
After Jimmy Giuffre

Pylon meadows and grazing horses

the flooded Breckland which we roll

past in the fog. Last year's reeds

are a skeletal army that gathers

in groups. One or two distant lights

shine far off from woods and deer

stand frozen watching us pass

the river leaves, comes back

leaves again as we enter the fens

Ten-Mile Bank runs off between lines

transporting the water out to sea

to the charge of white horses of the tides.

Auntie Heidi, haunter of boot sales

wearer of animal print jumpers

(Horses, always horses, sometimes dogs)

and a dirty laugh that could break glass

disappeared with her husband Phillip

along with his comb-over and gold tooth

down the Thanet Way to somewhere

near Herne Bay and we never heard

from them again. It was some imagined

slight that took them out of sight

and down the Medway to the sea. Cut noses

to spite faces. They'll be long dead now.

See how the unhappy dead

stand in groups watching us go,

they are clustered lights

in the deep woods,

they stand frozen watching us

pass, leave, return, leave again

only a river between us and them

but it's enough to make them distant

distant and skeletal, like pylons

we are running horses, all the pretty horses

black and bays, dapples and greys

and we are running free towards the sea.

SOMEWHERE TO GET TO

The light is growing in the East
the headlights skim the road
that runs beside the flooded fields
we're a month off blossom

when it comes I will drape
myself in the year's renewal
and ask how many times
I will see my little yard bloom

the need to weed the gaps between
the paving slabs and wall
peg out my children's clothes
and breathe in the warm cotton

the absence of the little bodies
from the house and the yard
calling to me from the cool
interiors of rooms where we live

our winter days are ending

and soon the plants will grow

and fill the empty patches

of earth and wood and field

my father would have been ninety

this spring and the birds would

sing to him as they sang to him

that foggy day he slipped away

and vanished over fences and walls

and kept going forever without

much to take with him on such

a distance that he undertook by foot

of course, he didn't walk anywhere

but I don't think that matters a deal

in the balance of things and truth

he went somewhere even if it was nowhere

really at all that could be mapped

or visited during the holidays

it has to be found in other ways

when the dead come to us in sleep

I can visit in my dreams, it is England

and there is a pub on a green

where we share a pint in the light

of a spring day and son, he says

son it's alright and we got that pint

we promised ourselves under blossom

and ghost birds sing from ghost

branches and no ghost cars come past

to climb the green hill beyond the trees

we change gear instead and I return

to this little swaying train compartment,

that runs beside the mirrored sky

and I look at all the empty seats

that will slowly fill as we stop

at fenland towns to collect the living

who always have something to do

and somewhere they must get to.

ACKNOWLEDGEMENTS

'Devotional for a Problem of Masculinity' (p8) and 'Devotional for fatherhood' first appeared in *Masculinity: An Anthology of Modern Voices* (Broken Sleep Books, 2024)

'Devotional for an iron bridge' first appeared in *The Rialto* #101 simply titled 'Iron Bridge' (2024)

'Devotional for the Acle Straight' first appeared in *Before the Dreadful Daylight Starts – An Anthology of Norfolk Poetry* (2023, Waterland Books) and later was featured in *Ten Poems from Norfolk* (Candlestick Press, 2025)

'Devotional for a dead hedgehog' and 'Devotional for masculinity' (p24) first appeared in *Lighthouse* #22 (Gatehouse Press, 2021)

The quotation by Cynthia Cruz is from her 2021 book The Melancholia of Class which is published by Repeater Books.

Thanks to Tiffany Atkinson, Martin Figura, Jo Guthrie, Andrea Holland, Helen Ivory, Esther Morgan for the Butchery workshops, and Roz Counelis, Matthew Gregory, Chandramohan Sathyanathan, Vincent De Souza, George Szirtes and Cat Woodward for the Take Five workshops. Your feedback helped me shape this book. Thanks also to Cameron Self and to Jeremy Noel-Tod.

LAY OUT YOUR UNREST